Joseph and His Brothers

First published in 1999 by Franklin Watts
96 Leonard Street, London EC2A 4RH

Franklin Watts Australia
14 Mars Road
Lane Cove
NSW 2066

Series editor: Rachel Cooke
Art director: Robert Walster
Consultants: Reverend Richard Adfield;
Laurie Rosenberg, Board of Deputies of British Jews

A CIP catalogue record for this book
is available from the British Library.

ISBN 0 7496 3215 1

Dewey Classification 221

Printed in Hong Kong/China

Joseph and His Brothers

Retold by Mary Auld

Illustrated by Diana Mayo

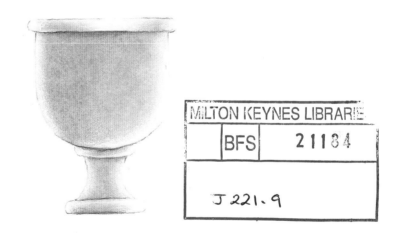

W

FRANKLIN WATTS

NEW YORK • LONDON • SYDNEY

There once was a man called Jacob who lived in the land of Canaan. Jacob had twelve sons and one daughter. His sons looked after his flocks of sheep in the hills and valleys around his home.

Of all his sons, Jacob loved his eleventh son, Joseph, the best, because he had been born when Jacob was growing old. Joseph worked alongside his brothers and told Jacob what they did wrong. And Jacob gave his favourite son a beautiful coat, decorated with many different colours.

Joseph's brothers were jealous. They
hated Joseph and were unkind to him.
They became even angrier when
Joseph told them of his amazing
dreams. In one, his brothers' sheaves of
corn bowed down to Joseph's; and in
another dream, the sun, the moon and

eleven stars bowed down to Joseph as
well. Did the dreams mean that Joseph
would one day be more important than
the rest of his family? Would they have
to bow to him like a king? His brothers
didn't like Joseph's dreams, and they
hated him all the more.

One day, Joseph set out to join his brothers, who were with their flocks far from home. The brothers saw Joseph coming: "Look, it's the dreamer. Let's kill him and see what comes of his dreams!" So they grabbed Joseph, ripped off his coat and threw him into a dry pit to die.

Soon after some merchants passed by, their camels laden with spices to be sold in Egypt. "Let's sell Joseph rather than kill him," suggested one plotter. "He is our brother after all!" So they sold Joseph as a slave to the merchants, for twenty pieces of silver.

The brothers tore up Joseph's coat and
covered it with goat's blood, and took it
to their father. Jacob was heartbroken:
Joseph had clearly been torn to pieces
by a wild animal. Nothing his family
said could comfort him.

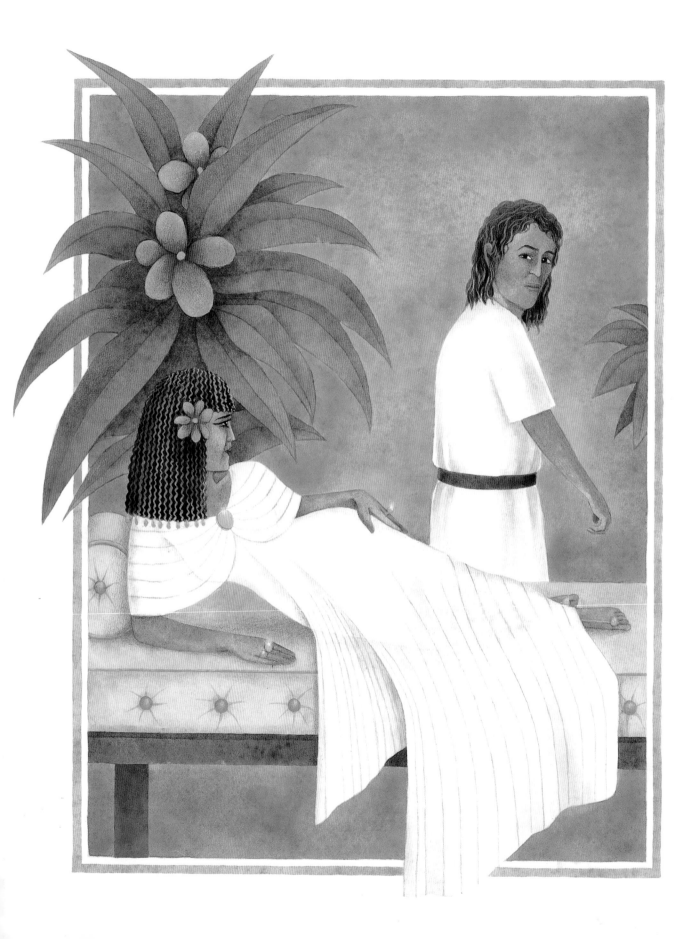

When the merchants arrived in Egypt, they sold Joseph to an Egyptian called Potiphar, a rich and important officer in the court of Pharaoh, king of Egypt. He liked Joseph, who worked hard for him, and soon put him in charge of his whole household. God was looking after Joseph.

All was going well until Potiphar's wife became interested in Joseph. He was very handsome and she wanted him to be her lover. Again and again she asked him but Joseph always refused. How could he betray his master? How could he sin against God?

Potiphar's wife grew angry. She went to her husband and told him Joseph had tried to kiss her and more. Potiphar was furious. He had Joseph thrown instantly into prison.

Even in prison, God watched over Joseph, for it was there he met two of Pharaoh's servants, his butler and his baker, who had got into trouble with their master.

One morning, Joseph found the two men in great distress. They had both had strange dreams in the night and were sure they must mean something. First the butler told his story. "I dreamt that I stood in front of a vine laden with ripe grapes. And I took the grapes and pressed them in Pharaoh's wine cup and gave the cup to him, and he drank all the wine."

With the help of God, Joseph
explained the butler's dream. "Pharaoh
will soon forgive you. You will be freed
and once again give Pharaoh his cup."

Now the baker told his dream. "I dreamt that I had baskets of bread on my head to take to Pharaoh, but before I could give them to him, some birds ate all the bread."

This dream was not so good. "Pharaoh will have your head chopped off," Joseph told the unhappy baker. And within three days, both dreams had come true. The butler was once again at Pharaoh's side and the baker was dead.

Back at his work, the butler forgot all about Joseph, even though Joseph had begged him for help. But then something happened to remind him: Pharaoh had been dreaming, two extraordinary dreams, and no one, not even his wisest magician, could tell him what they meant. Joseph was summoned to the court.

His hair cut and with new clothes, Joseph stood before Pharaoh. "It is not I, but God who will tell you the meaning of your dreams," he said.

So Pharaoh began: "I dreamt I was standing by the Nile, when seven strong, well-fed cows came out of the river and began to feed. Then seven more cows appeared, but they were thin

and scrawny - uglier than I have ever seen. And these skinny cows ate up the fat ones, but stayed as thin as before.

"Then I dreamt a second dream. This time seven ears of good, ripe corn grew up, but then seven more ears grew, shrivelled and windswept, and they swallowed up the good corn. Can you tell me what no other man has known?"

"Your dreams mean the same thing," said Joseph. "The seven fat cows and the healthy ears of corn are seven years of plenty when Egypt will have good harvests. The seven skinny cows and the shrivelled ears are seven years of terrible famine, which will follow.

"This is caused by God," explained Joseph. "You must appoint a wise man to prepare for the famine by organising food to be stored during the seven years of good harvest."

Pharaoh was impressed. "With the knowledge God has given you, there is surely none so wise as you," he said to Joseph. "You are the man to prepare Egypt for the famine. Only I shall be more powerful than you." And he gave Joseph his ring and fine linen to wear, and put a gold chain around his neck.

And, as Joseph had predicted, there were seven years of good harvests and then came awful famine, which spread throughout the world. Only in Egypt was there enough food for everyone because Joseph had made sure that there was plenty of grain in store.

In Canaan, Joseph's family
was starving. "You must go to
Egypt and buy some grain,"
Jacob told his remaining sons. So
Joseph's brothers set out for Egypt.
Only Benjamin, Joseph's youngest
brother, stayed behind.

Joseph controlled the sale of grain in Egypt, so it was to him the brothers went. They bowed low before the Pharaoh's magnificent officer - they did not realise it was Joseph at all. But Joseph recognised them, and he remembered his dreams.

Joseph decided to test his brothers. He gave them grain but made them promise to return to Egypt with Benjamin to prove they were trustworthy. He would keep one brother captive until they returned.

At first, Jacob would not let Benjamin go. He was terrified that he would lose him as he had lost Joseph. But eventually the famine forced him to allow his sons to return to Egypt.

This time Joseph gave his brothers a
splendid welcome. There was a great
feast and the brothers' sacks were filled
with grain. Secretly, Joseph told his
servants to hide a silver cup in
Benjamin's sack. Then he sent his
brothers on their way. Still none of
them had recognised him.

The brothers had not gone far when
Joseph sent his servants after them.
They searched the sacks and found
Joseph's precious cup in Benjamin's
grain. "Our master will make you
his slave for this theft," warned one
servant and they took the brothers
back to Joseph's house.

The brothers begged Joseph for mercy. "Our father has already lost one son. Without Benjamin, he will surely die. Take me as your slave instead!" offered one brother.

Joseph could no longer hold back. In tears, he told his brothers who he was. They were speechless. What would Joseph do to them?

"Don't worry," he said. "God has

wished it this way. If I hadn't come to Egypt, we would all have died in the famine. Now I can provide for us all - you must bring all our family to Egypt."

So Jacob and his family came to Egypt, as God had planned. Joseph met his father and embraced him. Father and son stayed in each other's arms for a long time. Egypt was now home to them both.

About this story

Joseph and His Brothers is a retelling of part of Genesis, the first book of the Bible. The Bible is the name given to the collection of writings that are sacred, in different forms, to the Jewish and Christian religions. Genesis, which means 'beginning', is the first of the 39 books in the Hebrew Bible, Tanakh, or Christian Old Testament. Genesis is also part of the Torah, the most sacred text of the Jewish religion.

Who was Joseph?

Joseph was the eleventh son of Jacob and the elder of two sons he had with Rachel, his favourite wife. The other was Benjamin, Jacob's twelfth and youngest son. Jacob, along with his father, Isaac, and his grandfather, Abraham, was one of the Patriarchs, or fathers, to whom the Hebrew people traced their ancestry and the start of the Jewish religion.

The chosen people

Genesis tells how God chose the Patriarchs and their families to be His people. God called Jacob Israel, which means 'to struggle to understand God'. Jacob's family and descendants, the Hebrews, were called the Children of Israel. In turn the Hebrews eventually formed the nation of Israel. Joseph himself had two sons, Ephraim and Manasseh, who were counted amongst the fathers of the twelve tribes of Israel (the other fathers were sons of Jacob).

From Genesis to Exodus

It is hard to give an exact date to when Joseph and his family arrived in Egypt from Canaan. It was probably in the 17th century BC, some 400 years before the events of Exodus, the next book of the Bible. In Exodus, the Hebrews are enslaved by a Pharaoh who did not know Joseph and then

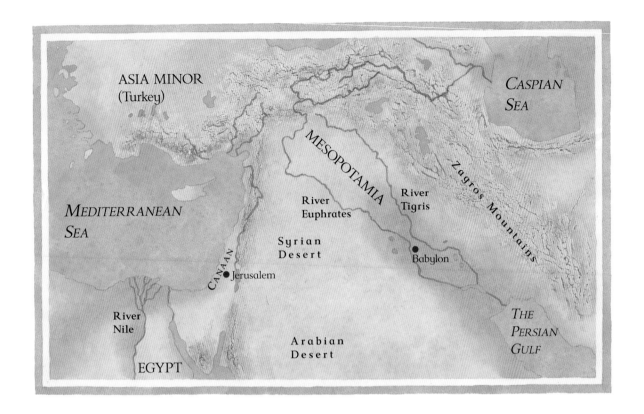

led out of slavery by Moses back to Canaan (the Promised Land). The story of Joseph provides a strong link between the Hebrew Patriarchs and the later history of the Hebrews under Moses.

God's purpose

One of the important themes of Genesis is how God protects His chosen people and ensures their long-term well-being. In the story of Joseph, God not only plans Joseph's move to Egypt but also makes sure that he does well there. In particular, it is God who helps Joseph interpret dreams so successfully. By the end of the story, God's purpose is clear. He has brought Jacob and his family to Egypt to protect them from the famine. He has also prepared the way forward for their descendants, the children of Israel, to be revealed to us in the next chapter of their history, Exodus.

Useful words

Betray If people trust you and you do something wrong and hurtful that they would not like, we say you have betrayed their trust.

Famine A famine occurs when there is very little food available and many people go hungry and starve. Famine is often the result of a natural disaster, such as a drought, when crops cannot grow because there is no rain.

Jealous When you feel jealous, you want something that belongs to someone else and, because you have not got it, you feel angry and envious of that person.

Magician A magician is someone who knows about and performs magic. In ancient times, people took magic very seriously and believed that it could explain many things in life they did not understand. A magician was seen as a wise and knowledgeable man, not just someone who did tricks.

Merchant A merchant is someone who makes a living by buying and selling things, or goods. A merchant often takes the goods over long distances, buying them cheaply in one place and selling them for more money in another.

Mercy To show mercy is to hold back from punishing someone for doing something wrong. It is kind to show mercy and is a part of forgiving.

Pharaoh Pharaoh is the name given to the kings of ancient Egypt.

Sheaves Sheaves are bundles of corn (wheat). In the past, when corn was harvested by hand, it was tied into sheaves to store it.

Sin To sin is to do something bad and wicked, which makes God unhappy and goes against the laws of religion.

What do you think?

These are some questions about *Joseph and His Brothers* to ask yourself and to talk about with other people.

How would you have felt about Joseph if you were one of his brothers?

What do you think Joseph felt when his brothers sold him into slavery?

Why would Joseph have betrayed Potiphar if he did what Potiphar's wife asked?

After he left prison, how well did the butler behave towards Joseph?

How do you think it would feel to live through a famine?

Why didn't Jacob want Benjamin to go to Egypt?

Why do you think Joseph was crying when he told his brothers who he was?

How do you think Jacob and Joseph felt when they were reunited?

Does Joseph's story remind you of any other Bible stories you know?

What does this story of Joseph show us about God?